Total **Restoration**

Jean-Ronel Corbier, M.D.

Michelle Corbier, M.D.

Total *Restoration*

Jean-Ronel Corbier, M.D.

Michelle Corbier, M.D.

© 2004 by Dr. Jean-Ronel Corbier & Dr. Michelle Corbier. All rights reserved.

Printed in the United States of America

No part of this publication may be reproduced, stored in a retrieval system, or transmitted in any way by any means—electronic, mechanical, photocopy, recording, or otherwise—without the prior permission of the copyright holder, except as provided by USA copyright law.

Scripture references are taken from the King James Version of the Bible.

Scripture taken from the HOLY BIBLE, NEW INTERNATIONAL VERSION®. NIV®. Copyright©1973, 1978, 1984 by International Bible Society. Used by permission of Zondervan. All rights reserved.

Published by:
Ufomadu Consulting & Publishing
P.O. Box 746
Selma, AL 36702-0746

ISBN 0-9754197-4-9
Library of Congress Catalog Card Number: 2004195455

Acknowledgments

We thank Jesus Christ in all things at all times. We thank Him for allowing us to share this message with others.

Table of Contents

Chapter 1- Introduction   13
Chapter 2- Biblical perspectives on the origin of Illness   19
Chapter 3 -Restoration and healing in the Bible   27
Chapter 4- Explanation of the RESTORATION model   33
Chapter 5- Practical application of the RESTORATION
         model: Prescription for health and healing   61
Chapter 6- Conclusion   91

Preface

Medical science has come a long way. Our diagnostic capabilities are incredible and our ability to intervene acutely in complex situations is unsurpassed. Technological advances coupled with the commitment to state-of-the-art research have caused our current medical system to become supreme. Despite our medical technological breakthroughs all is not well. Many chronic illnesses are on the rise. The cost of health care is staggering. Many people are dissatisfied and feel helpless. Is there any reason for people to have hope if the medical experts say that there is nothing that can be done for a particular problem? What if you are heavily medicated and still are not experiencing any significant relief? What if you are after a cure instead of palliation of symptoms?

We have written this book to answer these and many other questions that people are asking today. From our collective experience as doctors, we marvel at medical science, but, at the same time we clearly see its flaws. We are Christian physicians who believe that ultimate healing comes from God. Instead of our Christian faith being challenged by current medical knowledge, it has instead been strengthened. We believe that there is an important role for such concepts as prayer and faith. With that acknowledgement, total restoration from illness and disease is possible. The challenge is to understand how to combine the best of the current medical system with a deep understanding of mental, biological and spiritual factors when it comes to health and illness.

We draw our source of inspiration from Jeremiah 30: 17 "But I will *restore* you to health and heal your wounds, declares the Lord".

Chapter 1 - Introduction

Throughout history, man has tried to find solutions for infirmities and ways to delay death. He has searched for various cures and therapeutic interventions to combat disease and illness. In the Bible, healing is associated with God. A review of history shows how healing eventually became identified with the 'gods'. People started searching for healing from the religious elite, the priests. There was still a connection made however between healing and deity.

In time, man started associating healing with knowledge. With the development of the germ theory man believed that because he could 'see' the object which caused disease that he could eradicate it. All healing was based upon *his* knowledge. Healing, therefore, did not require divine intervention. Man was all powerful and could affect his own future. With the age of science, powerful drugs were manufactured. Antibiotics, vaccines, pain killers, sedatives… we created drugs to defeat illness.

Total Restoration

Along with medical *enlightenment*, came the Industrial Age. Man moved off the farms and into the cities. Less people were available to produce the crops to feed the masses. No problem for man. Man discovered how to farm crops in mass quantities. The techniques designed to harvest crops in large quantities were harmful though. This destructive farming, unfortunately, destroyed our farmlands during the Dustbowl. In 1931, drought destroyed over ploughed and overgrazed lands. Farms had been depleted of important nutrients and farmed improperly to yield greater crops. About 100 million acres lost their topsoil by 1934.

But man supposedly learned from his mistakes. We then began using chemicals, DDT, and other pesticides, to 'protect' our crops. We now have to pick our crops earlier because the produce has to travel farther to get to the world market. We also use chemicals to help our produce look more appealing. As a result of these techniques we now find that our fruits and vegetables are less nutritious.

So now, not only does man feel omniscient (knows it all) and omnipotent (all powerful), he has found a way to enhance the appeal of

Introduction

his crops in a way that is also very profitable commercially. Now man can relax and become sedentary. Man stopped 'working by the sweat of his brow' to get his food. God never intended for us to be sedentary or else he would not have created us with over 600 muscles, whose main purpose is movement.

We now join clubs to 'work out' since natural exercise is no longer part of our daily routine. Some of us do not even take the time to work out. As the saying goes 'if you don't use it – you lose it'. Arthritis, slipped capital femoral epiphysis, carpal tunnel and osteoarthritis are all disorders related to inactivity, repetitive limited activity and obesity. Obesity is the sin of indulgence. This was once the disease of the affluent. But today, fast food and TV dinners has made obesity an equal opportunity killer. The average American eats 149 lbs of sugar per year. In one year, we consume the amount of sugar that our ancestors ate in their lifetime! So, where are we now…

Dissatisfaction and dismay with the current medical establishment has led people to re-evaluate the origin of illness. People are looking at any and everything to cure them of their infirmities. Dissatisfied patients are asking their doctors for things to heal them without the side effects or costs of traditional drugs. People are also looking into alternative therapies for healing. One of these alternative methods includes herbal therapies. Much money and time is devoted to this investigation. What people have forgotten is that many drugs come from plants! Research companies are well aware of this fact though. They spend millions of dollars traveling around the world, even into the ocean, in search of plants to create their next 'wonder drug'. So, if we make drugs from plants to heal our infirmities, why not just use the plants themselves to heal our infirmities. Why not de-emphasize the drugs, and the drug companies. Why not focus on the consumption of fruits and vegetables in their natural state, as the Lord originally intended.

Herbal treatment and other forms of interventions that do not rely on synthetic drugs are often called alternative therapies. People are choosing non- pharmaceutical options to avoid the problem of side effects and to address the underlying health problems instead of simply masking their symptoms. It is a fact that there are over 100, 000 deaths per year attributed to **properly** prescribed drugs and another 2.2

Introduction

million serious adverse effects occur. In addition, for many individuals drugs may simply be ineffective. Thus, people are looking for ways to heal themselves naturally. Where can we get these natural therapies? They can be obtained in plants where God has always put them. Unfortunately, our plants today have fewer nutrients than before. We, therefore, have to endeavor to find organic fruits and vegetables. We are still obligated today to supplement our diets with essential nutrients in order to attain optimal health; examples include antioxidants, essential fatty acids, glyconutrients, minerals, phytochemicals, trace elements, and vitamins. Even the American Medical Association (AMA) has advised people that it is prudent to take vitamin supplementation. Daily, medical studies are showing the benefits of antioxidants, essential fatty acids and other supplements. Our current diets are not sufficient to provide the nutrients we need to be healthy. Our diets are in fact contributing to a lot of the chronic disorders that were once rare but have now reached epidemic proportions.

Radical changes are necessary in order to prevent the downward spiral of disease. A

Total Restoration

fresh new approach is in order. But what options do we have? Where do we look?

Chapter 2 - Biblical perspectives on the Origin of Illness

In the beginning God made Adam and Eve. They were perfect and without sin or illness. In Genesis 2:15, The Lord God took the man and put him in the Garden of Eden to work it, and take care of it. And the Lord God commanded the man, 'you are free to eat from any tree in the garden.' In Genesis 1: 29, God told Adam and Eve: "I give you every seed-bearing plant on the face of all the whole earth and every tree that has fruit with seed in it. They will be yours for food." God's original diet for man included fruits and vegetables. After creating man, He gave him an *operator's manual* or set of instructions pertaining to his nutritional requirements. He knew, and still knows, the importance plants play in health and healing. We find in fruits and vegetables, all kinds of essential nutrients, live enzymes, fiber and water needed for optimal health. This was man's original diet.

But man grieved the Lord, and sinned to the point were God stated "My spirit will not contend with man forever… his days will be 120 years" Genesis 6:3. Although curtailed, those years were supposed to be active, productive years. The life of Abraham stands as an example of a life of faithfulness to God, and obedience to His laws. Abraham traveled extensively, usually by foot. He was physically very active, even engaging in military combat with his enemies. He had many children, and continued to have children even after 100 years of age. Abraham did not have dementia or Alzheimer's. He did not have heart disease of diabetes. He lived in his own home with his *second* wife until his death. He did not live in a nursing home with hospice in attendance.

In contrast to Abraham is his son Isaac. Isaac had inherited the riches of his father. Though he traveled some and probably labored a little, he lived a life of privilege provided by the labors of his father. Isaac had twin sons by Rebekah, his wife. The boys were of very different temperaments. Jacob loved to attend sheep, and was of a quiet and gentle nature. Esau was a more active and volatile personality. Esau loved to hunt game. He would often bring his kill home to prepare for his father to eat. We see from the scriptures that Isaac had a love

Biblical Perspectives on the Origin of Illness

of meats. In Genesis 25:28 the scripture states "Isaac who had a taste for wild game, loved Esau, but Rebekah loved Jacob." Further in Genesis we are told that Isaac's eyes "were so weak that he could no longer see." I wonder if Isaac may have developed type 2 diabetes from his indulgent diet. We see very often today, how people who have rich diets, high in saturated fats develop diabetes. Diabetes is also the #1 cause of blindness for adults in America, according to the National Institutes of Health. Diabetic retinopathy is a disease that is completely related to diet and afflicts many people today. Here we see an example of how a diet opposed to God's plan can lead to disease and illness.

Man chose to continue to disobey God. This led to degeneration of our bodies and mind. In their deteriorated state, men became susceptible to illness and disease. Despite their sins, the Lord continued to be with His people. He had promised Abraham to bless his offspring, that they would be more numerous than the sands on the seashore as seen in Genesis 22:17 "I will surely bless you and make your descendants as numerous as the stars in the sky and as the sand on the seashore." But the descendants of Abraham would be sorely tested in their faith and obedience to God's laws. After fleeing the famine in Canaan, the Israelites took refuge in Egypt. There they were enslaved. The Lord continued to be with the children of Israel, especially after their enslavement in Egypt. The Lord provided for their sustenance. While fleeing through the desert the Lord told Moses; 'I will rain down bread from heaven for you.'

Manna was to be a complete food for the children of Israel. It was so important that the Lord commanded that some manna be placed in the ark of the covenant. Hebrews 9:3 'this ark contained the gold jar of manna, Aaron's staff that had budded, and the stone tablets of the covenant." The Lord also made sure that the people had sufficient water along their journey to the Promised Land. But the people grumbled against Moses. They were not content to simply have the manna. They longed for the foods of the Egyptians. To appease their appetites the Lord sent quail to them also. He promised to provide for their daily needs, but some of the people horded the food and kept it over night despite the commands of the Lord.

The food that was hidden over night became contaminated with maggots and was rotten in the morning. The Lord was trying to enforce the concept of temperance. They only needed enough food to eat to meet the daily physical needs of their bodies. Today, we see people who live to eat, instead of eating to live. This indulgence of the appetite leads to obesity, diabetes, hypertension, gastritis and a multitude of other illnesses.

The Lord would not stop there. He had many other health laws to share with His children. He promised to not bring the illnesses of the Egyptians upon them if they remained obedient to His laws of health. Leviticus 26:11-12 shows God's promise to dwell among the people of Israel if they were obedient 'I will put my dwelling place among you, and I will not abhor you, I will walk among you and be your God, and you will be my people." Through out the book of Leviticus the Lord gives His children health laws. The Lord even told His children how to treat the land that grew their food, Leviticus 25: 2-7. Many people find these laws obtrusive and unnecessary. Whether you chose to abide by these laws or not, the Lord's purpose in creating these laws was not to add a burden for the children of Israel, but to free them from a life of servitude to disease and illness.

Total Restoration

By being healthy they would be an example to others showing how obedience to God gives a good long vibrant life. Being healthy would give them the ability to serve God and to witness to others. If you are always sick, it is hard to be a servant of God and do His work. God does not wish for anyone to be ill. Illness is a result of sin. The sin may not be the result of one person's sin, but the result of living in a sinful world. We all need to do all we can, though, to be well. And wellness is possible through obedience to God's health laws.

God explained to the children of Israel how He wanted them to be a *special* people. He wanted them to be witnesses to the world of His love and faithfulness. They were to be faithful and love Him. They were to obey His laws. The Lord, in His mercy, warned His children of the results of failure to obey these laws. In Leviticus 26:15-16 "… and if you reject my decrees and abhor my laws and fail to carry out all my commands and so violate my covenant, then I will do this to you: I will bring upon you sudden terror, wasting diseases and fever that will destroy your sight and drain away your life." Illness is a choice. Likewise, we must choose to follow the path of wellness, although this may take a concerted effort.

Chapter 3- Restoration and healing in the Bible

We see throughout the Bible how God would heal people and use things in nature to effect that healing. In 2Kings 5:10-14 we see Naaman was told to cleanse himself in the Jordan River. Initially, the proud Naaman was incensed that the prophet Elisha would direct him to cleanse himself in the dirty river of Jordan. He left disappointed and angry. He would easily kill a hundred soldiers to obtain healing. Naaman could pay Elisha untold wealth to get healing. But to simply obey the word of God, through his prophet Elisha, seemed too hard for this mighty man, Naaman. After being counseled by his servants, Naaman obeyed the prophet, and was healed. God does not need nor want our money. God only asks us to obey Him, and He will heal us, in His good time.

We often see people in our office with children who are severely ill and afflicted. They tell us how much money they have spent, and the distances they have traveled to obtain healing for their children. Sometimes God has to humble us in order for His work to be done in us. Only when we surrender everything, including ourselves, will God work His miracles in us. He can heal us without our consent, but that would not be a God who gives His children a choice. We have the choice of life or death. We also have a choice between illness and healing.

In the story of Hezekiah, as told in 2 Kings 20:1-7, the Lord healed Hezekiah of his boil. The Lord directed Hezekiah to apply a poultice of figs to the boil for the healing to occur. Figs are significant in the Bible and throughout history. In Genesis 3:7 we see that after their sin, Adam and Eve used the leaves from the fig tree to cover their nakedness. Figs were noted to be beneficial to effect healing. Pliny of Rome stated, 'Figs are restorative". Figs contain fiber, soluble and insoluble, iron, calcium and antioxidants. God chose the figs purposefully. Figs have natural healing powers. But why did the Lord chose the fig? Did the fig cause the healing or did God? God does not need the fig tree, or any other item to effect His healing. He used the fig tree because Hezekiah needed it. Hezekiah needed to have something tangible

Restoration and Healing in the Bible

to see the healing power of God. God is so merciful that He meets us where we are in our faith. Because without faith there cannot be healing. Jesus often said, 'Your faith has made you whole'. Without faith, God will not heal us.

Sometimes when God heals us, he also bestows upon us further blessings. In the case of Hezekiah, God stated "And I will add unto thy days fifteen years; and I will deliver thee and this city out of the hand of the king of Assyria." 2 Kings 20:6. Hezekiah only prayed for the healing of his boil and the removal of the sentence of death upon himself. But God had even more planned for him. God loves us, and wants us to thrive, not just to survive. The blessings the Lord wishes to share with His children are innumerable; we only need to claim these blessings in the name of Jesus Christ.

In the New Testament we see an example of Jesus' healing with the story of the blind man. In Mark 8:22-25 we see Jesus healing the blind man. Jesus spit on the man's eyes and then placed His hands upon the man. The man was able to see some things initially, but then Jesus placed His hands upon the man's eyes. The scripture then

Total Restoration

states that the man was "restored, and saw every man clearly". Why would the Lord spit upon a person's eyes? The disgust this process raises to a person's mind is obvious. I remember first reading this verse and thinking, could not the Lord heal Him just with the touch? What is the significance of the spit? Well, saliva has healing properties of its own. We have enzymes and antibodies that protect our mouth and gut from harmful organisms. By using these things we possess, either in our physical bodies or in nature to cause us to be healed, the Lord is showing us the potential for healing that surrounds us each day.

God has provided for us abundantly on this home we call earth. He knows what we need each day to be healed. He provided us with those things we need to be healed and restored to full and vibrant health. The Lord wants us to be healed. Only by being healed can we be fully capable of doing the Lord's work. But we can also be a testimony to others of God's healing abilities when we are healed and freed from our afflictions.

In Jeremiah 8:22 the question is asked "Is there no balm in Gilead; is there no physician there? Why then is not the health of the daughter of my people recovered?"

Restoration and Healing in the Bible

The answer is given by further reading. Jeremiah 9:13 "And the Lord saith, because they have forsaken my law which I set before them, and have not obeyed my voice, neither walked therein." The people were being punished for their disobedience to God's laws. Further, Jeremiah 9:23-24 states: "Let not the wise man glory in his wisdom, neither let the mighty man glory in his might, let not the rich man glory in his riches: But let him that glorieth glory in this, that he understandeth and knoweth me, that I am the Lord which exercise loving kindness, judgment, and righteousness, in the earth: for in these things I delight, saith the Lord." The Lord wants us to adhere to the health principles He so lovingly provided for us. This obedience should not be simply born out of duty, but from love. God has given us directions about certain foods to eat, or not to eat, which could provide us with an amazing amount of healing if only we would obey these laws.

Unfortunately, what happens when we hear the word law? We immediately resist. There is something innate to humans, which makes us object instantly to the word law or rule. The Lord did not provide health laws to be a burden to His children, but to be a means of freeing them – from illness and disease.

Chapter 4- Definition of the Restoration Model

Is healing possible today? What about the health care system? How does one combine medical and alternative health care principles in a sensible way? We have at the beginning of the book stated that we see limitations with the current health care system, although it has progressed significantly through the years. Let us look at this system more closely:

❖ The current medical system is biologically based.

Biology is important in understanding illness, but it is just one among many components. It is important in the establishment and treatment of disease. A biological approach seeks to understand and treat diseases by identifying biological disturbances that may be present. These biological disturbances are tangible, verifiable and, hopefully, modifiable. Drugs play a crucial role in this system in that their use is predicated on treatment of biochemical dysfunctions thought to be associated with a particular disease process. At least 5oo molecular targets have been identified for drugs to do their work.

Drugs do work and a lot of research supports their use and also provides an explanation of their pharmacokinetic and pharmacodynamic properties. It becomes very easy to rely on drugs for everything though. Since we live in an era where we love comfort and ease and are inpatient, it becomes obvious why a drug has been developed for virtually every medical, mental or psychiatric condition.

A biologically-based approach works very well if an illness is: primarily biological in origin, if a laboratory investigation exists which can prove the existence of the defect, if a treatment option is available that is safe for the particular individual, and if the problem once properly treated does not recur. Unfortunately, a very large number of conditions do not fit these parameters.

Definition of the Restoration Model

There are many conditions that appear biological but are mostly psychogenic (mental-based) or stress-related. A good example that I have encountered in both adults and children are refractory seizures that do not respond to seizure medication. The seizures are later discovered to be caused by stress or psychogenic factors.

Because many problems are stress-related, they may not have biological markers even when they may present convincingly as a biological disorder. In these cases, very expensive tests are repeated over and over again, the physician (usually a specialist) may conclude that the particular illness is 'in the head' in that it 'is not real or organic.' Worst of all, the patient may be told: 'there is nothing that we can do'. If the individual has gone to a variety of medical institutions and has been seen by leading specialists, spending a lot of money, that individual may start to despair and believe that there is no hope. Biologically-based paradigms are therefore limiting.

Total Restoration

- ❖ The current medical system is reductionistic.

    All illness is evaluated by trying to look for the smallest sub-unit of dysfunction. You first look at the entire organism, then decide what organ system is involved (e.g. nervous system versus rheumatologic, gastrointestinal, endocrine, etc). If it is an eye problem, you can no longer rely on the ophthalmologist; you may eventually have to see a retina specialist, a cornea specialist, a lens specialist, a neuro-ophthalomologist, etc. The study of the eyeball has become remarkably subspecialized, as if it were not specialized enough. Beyond the organ system, you then have to narrow it down to the specific organ, (e.g. brain, heart, pancreas, bone, etc.). Then you can finally start to think about which tissues are involved such as the mucosa, gray matter, islets of langerhans, etc. From there, you can delve into the cell to determine which subcellular structures or organelles are affected (for example, the mitochondria, the peroxisomes, the

Definition of the Restoration Model

Golgi apparatus or lysosomes). It does not really end there. You may actually be able to determine which part of the mitochondria accounts for the child in front of you who has seizures, weakness, fatigue, hyperactive, mood swings, malnourishment and defiance. If you have a complex medical problem and you are referred to one, two or ten specialists and no one can help you, then you have a big problem. At least you have a big insurmountable problem based on the conventional model.

❖ The current medical system is symptom-based.

For many conditions, the goal is to control the symptoms instead of treating the underlying cause. If you have migraine headaches, for instance, the reflex therapeutic approach is to use abortive and prophylactic drugs instead of focusing on life-style issues that may be causing the headaches. As mentioned earlier, there is a medication for everything, as if every condition were caused by a particular medication deficiency. This is not to say there is no role for drugs. There are various acute situations where drugs can be lifesaving. There is, however, an over reliance on drugs for conditions that are purely life-style related and that can safely and completely be corrected. It seems that for many people, the symptom-based approach works well since patients have become accustomed to expecting and sometimes demanding the magical pill, and the physician is happy to take the few seconds required to write the prescription instead of taking the time to discuss the cause of the problem. After all, time is money. Patients can continue to indulge and lead a disease-prone lifestyle since a pill is there to ease them through any discomfort associated with the disease they experience. In this situation, you can envision a *disease care* instead of *healthcare* system.

❖ The medical system is, therefore, palliative.

The manner in which individuals are treated suggests that the goal in many cases is palliative. Many patients are told that the cause of their condition is unkn0wn. For instance, individuals with autoimmune disorders are often told that they have an *idiopathic* condition (cause

Definition of the Restoration Model

unknown). The various complaints are treated symptomatically, while the patient is informed that they have a chronic, life-long condition. A patient is never told: "here is what we are going to do to cure your condition" despite all of the advances in medicine. Surgery is sometimes considered curative but may not always solve the problem as far as the initial cause.

A different way to look at health and illness is through the RESTORATION model. It is a more dynamic model that is comprehensive and integrative.

The model is explained as follows:

- ❖ The RESTORATION model is based on an understanding of biopsychosociospiritual factors.

    o In addition to focusing on biological causes, the RESTORATION MODEL also looks at illness from psychological, social and spiritual perspectives. Illness is bi-directional. Biological disturbances can affect our mental wellbeing and secondarily disrupt our social milieu. This in turn can adversely affect our spirituality. The reverse is also true.

- A primarily spiritual problem can affect every aspect of our health including ones that are biologically based. A so-called "refractory" or "idiopathic" illness may not be so challenging and enigmatic if pychosociospiritual factors are considered. Although a greater acceptance and appreciation of psychosocial factors has occurred in the past few years, spiritual concerns are still poorly understood and often ignored.

- Medical doctors have been trained to view illness as a biological disorder. Theories about the specific cause of the dysfunction and treatment strategies leave little room for spiritual factors. I say "little room" because in recent years, the Diagnostic and Statistical Manual of Mental Disorders 4th edition (the official clinical

Definition of the Restoration Model

manual published by the American Psychiatric Association) has recognized the contribution of spiritual disturbances in illness. They even have a diagnostic code: **V62.89.** This code is used: *"when the focus of clinical attention is a religious or spiritual problem. Examples include distressing experiences that involve loss or questioning of faith, problems associated with conversion to a new faith, or questioning of spiritual values that may not necessarily be related to an organized church or religious institution."*

- Spirituality is crucial when it comes to illness. Factors such as faith, humility, love, peace and joy promote health while fear, guilt, chronic resentment and a desire for revenge are harmful to our health.

- All of these negative emotions may cause any or all of the following:
  - Impaired sleep
  - Impaired gastrointestinal function
  - Hypertension (high blood pressure)
  - Headaches
  - Anxiety symptoms
  - Mood disorders
  - Chronic pain syndromes
  - Fatigue
  - Impair memory and concentration

In addition, the above negative emotions can also adversely impact the immune system. If a person has additional risk factors, strokes and heart attacks may be precipitated and autoimmune disorders may develop.

So, let's say that instead of chronic fear and guilt someone decides to place their faith in God with the belief that He is all powerful,

Definition of the Restoration Model

you can see how that person's blood pressure may decrease. He may gain peace, happiness, joy, and all of the associated hormonal benefits.

Faith is also vital. It is interesting to note that Christ, when He was on earth, accomplished numerous miracles. He often would say 'your faith has made you whole', or has healed you. Faith must be important for Jesus to have made this statement repeatedly. Faith is more than belief. It is an active, dynamic process that allows an individual to have access to healing that would otherwise not be possible.

Before considering the importance of placing one's faith in God, one should consider the simple example of a **placebo response.** A placebo is an inert substance, a 'sugar pill' that when taken has a therapeutic response. A patient may experience a sort of therapeutic benefit from a pill if he believes that the pill will help him, even if the pill is inert. Placebos have helped in a variety of problems such as severe pain, stomach problems, headaches and even warts. Negative responses have also been noted and have been called **nocebos.** For instance, a teacher had students voluntarily participate in research by taking a *mood* pill. The teacher explained to the students the list of side effects which included: gastrointestinal symptoms (stomachache, nausea, vomiting), neurological disturbances (headache, dizziness) and sensory disturbances (blurred vision). Just as expected, several students experienced these side effects, sometimes severely. It was then explained to the students that the pill was really a sugar pill with no biological effect upon the body. The *expectation* that something bad could happen was enough to cause these students to actually develop adverse symptoms.

The placebo response is based on belief, and is very powerful. It can supercede the actual pharmacological effect of a drug. Several authors have shown that expectancy of a given effect can override the pharmacological effects. Despite the power of a placebo, faith is distinct from the placebo response. Although both are based on belief and anticipation, faith has an added element. Several studies have been conducted on the role of intercessory prayer for individuals with serious illnesses. These studies have been conducted in such prestigious institutions as Duke University and the Mayo Clinic. In several of the studies, the patients that were receiving prayer did not know that people were praying for them. The patients still did better than those patients that did not receive intercessory prayer. There are many examples in the Bible and also in the current society where other individuals expressed faith and prayed for an individual who was too sick to pray or have faith. These examples show that faith is not to be confused with a placebo response.

Forgiveness is also a very important spiritual component of illness. The ability to forgive or receive forgiveness can be associated with healing of some 'refractory' illnesses. Anthropologists have studied healing practices in lower Zaire (now called Congo in central Africa). They have found that a form of kinship therapy occurred where group reconciliation was

Definition of the Restoration Model

facilitated by an *ngunza* or prophet. It was interesting to note that reconciliation, forgiveness and confession were found to be associated with healing of illness. In the Bible, Jesus also uses the phrase: 'your sins are forgiven". Christ knew that for many individuals, healing could occur if the sick individual had the assurance that his sins were forgiven.

- ❖ Instead of reductionistic, the RESTORATION model is holistic.

  - o Full restoration is only possible if all factors that may be contributing to illness are taken into consideration. This includes biological, psychological, social and spiritual. In addition, total restoration as far as biology is concerned, requires an approach that works *with*, instead of against, the body. Covering up or suppressing a symptom with drugs is not the same as correcting a nutritional deficiency or avoiding food toxins that may be causing the problem in the first place.

- Imagine a person with chronic hypertension, lupus, diabetes or migraine headaches being told: 'Your condition is chronic, and life-long. We do not know why you have that problem. You will need to take these pills for the rest of your life. You better be compliant with taking this drug', instead of that person being told 'there are various problems that may be contributing to your condition including dietary, life style, stress and genetic predisposition. While we may not be able to alter you genes, there are many ways that we can help encourage your body's natural healing mechanisms or *the doctor within* by the grace of God. God is able to help you and I will do what I can to assist you'. Everything the body needs for proper functioning such as proper nutrition, proper hydration with water, exercise, good social and spiritual support, adequate rest, and temperance is vital not

Definition of the Restoration Model

only for maintenance of optimal wellness but also for the re-establishment of total health.

- ❖ The RESTORATION model is etiologic-based.
    - o Complete return to health cannot occur unless the underlying problem is addressed. The body has an innate healing mechanism that in some cases allows it to carry out its curative action, independent of medical intervention. A good example is a viral upper respiratory or ear infection for which an antibiotic (useless against viral infections) is prescribed for two weeks. After two weeks the individual gets better because the viral infection is terminated and overcome by the immune system. It so happens that the antibiotic was prescribed for the same length of time. A misinformed parent might thus sing the praises of a drug that did not do anything. People must realize that illness is not a medication

deficiency problem. A headache is not caused by ibuprofen deficiency any more than heart burn is caused by a ranitidine deficiency. Headaches can be caused by numerous factors, often nutrition and life style related, that could be easily corrected without medication.

- What about genes? Genes are indeed very important in the manifestation of most illnesses, but they are just one contributing factor. At best, genes may cause a greater susceptibility or vulnerability in an individual, but with proper life style, attitude, nutrition and some spiritual help, the genetic vulnerability may remain just that, a genetic vulnerability. Yes, when it comes to weight for instance, some people have to struggle more than others. Unlike my wife who can eat whatever she wants, whenever she wants and remain thin, it would seem that just looking at food makes me gain weight. Despite the fact that there are obese individuals on both

Definition of the Restoration Model

> sides of my family, I was able, by using the principles of the RESTORATION model, to lose 100 lbs and keep the weight off.
>
> o There is, in fact, no *sickness gene.* There are no genes that exist to cause disease; instead, when some genes are abnormally expressed or mutated, they can code for proteins that can then cause metabolic derangements that can result in illness.
>
> o In reality, if you look at all of the individuals that are taken to the doctor's office or the hospital and examine the actual cause of their disease, the etiology is often nutrition, life style or stress related. Statistically then, addressing these issues thoroughly should result in restoration of health for many.

❖ The RESTORATION model is curative.

> o Instead of palliative, our model is restorative. It is based on the understanding that total healing is possible, even though in some

cases it would take a miracle. In the tough cases, Divine intervention may be the only avenue to secure a cure. This model places no limitations on the possibility of healing, even for the most refractory cases. Healing is not predicated on diagnosis, chronicity, cause, genetic vulnerability, or virulence of the infection. Instead, the level of faith, prayer, and God's willingness to intervene are the most important factors. This model is one that should bring hope and comfort. Although a cure is never out of reach, a cure may not always be God's will. In a broad spiritual context, sometimes some good may come out of a person's afflictions. Good for the person, or others around them. The illness may be temporary. Someone who is going through a chronic illness and understands the RESTORATION model would be equipped to face the illness with a positive attitude and hope. Hope, by itself, may contribute to healing.

Definition of the Restoration Model

- One must always be willing to take responsibility for their actions. In many cases, violating some simple health laws may lead to illness, with secondary, tertiary and quaternary problems complicating health further. A miracle or Divine intervention should never be expected, if violations of health laws are not corrected and deliberately ignored.

The RESTORATION model is complete. In order for its application to have positive effects, it must be understood in its entirety. All of the principles in the model are important. The model cannot be fully effective if a few principles are applied and others are ignored. These principles work together. They are all interrelated. Applying all of the principles will cause synergistic results.

Chapter 5 - Practical application of the RESTORATION model: Prescription for health and healing

RESTORATION is also used as an acronym that describes very specifically the steps and factors needed to obtain a full return to health:

R – RENEWAL

"Create in me a pure heart, O God, and renew a steadfast spirit within me."
Ps 51:10

When it comes to complex and chronic medical problems, no real improvement can occur without a renewal of the mind. There needs to be a renewal of your attitude and approach toward wellness. A change in the very perception of one's illness as a conquerable problem may *already* initiate some very positive changes toward healing.

A renewal entails a complete change, a makeover, a total alteration. This is a type of change that can only come from God. Even with individuals who possess an inner strength to change, that willpower and inner strength are a gift from God. Many individuals, unfortunately, feel helpless and hopeless. Perhaps a very grim prognosis has been given to them, such as cancer. Or perhaps you may feel unable to get rid of excess weight. That is the time, more than ever, that a person needs to seek total renewal of mind and body. Below we list some very practical advice with respect to how a renewal is possible.

First, start with the recognition that there is a problem. Many individuals recognize that something is wrong only when symptoms fully manifest themselves. Individuals with serious health problems are caught up with all of the secondary issues pertaining to their illness but spend very little time reflecting on the nature their illness and its implications.

- ❖ Ask God for help. Ask God to bring a renewal. God is the author of all good things and is willing to provide help.
- ❖ One must be willing to surrender to God.
- ❖ One must start exercising faith. God is in control, always.
- ❖ A renewal requires being humble.

Definition of the Restoration Model

- ❖ Total renewal requires having a forgiving heart.
- ❖ A total renewal entails a full commitment for a lifestyle change.
- ❖ Avoid procrastination.
- ❖ It is important to remain focused, and not get distracted by negative thoughts or predictions.

E – EXERCISE

"Six days you shall labor and do all your work"
Exodus 20: 9

Exercise is vital. Some people have lifestyles or jobs that allow them to remain active automatically. For the rest of us, we must make time to exercise. There should absolutely be no excuse not to exercise. Whether you have a very hectic schedule or are bed-ridden, you should still exercise. You may need to start slowly and discuss an exercise program with your physician if you are unfit or have heart disease.

It is very important to understand that by exercising you are helping various aspects of bodily function including: your lymphatic system, metabolism, gastrointestinal system, weight control, immune system, and endocrine system. Exercise helps with detoxification. Detoxification allows elimination of harmful toxins from the body by using virtually every system in the body, including cutaneous, lymphatic, and respiratory.

In addition, you are also boosting many mental and spiritual functions as well. Exercise is a good way to fight stress and improve mood. For those who want a very simple exercise that can be continued lifelong with multiple benefits, we recommend the following:

- ❖ Walk for 1 hour, early, every morning at approximately the same time each day.
- ❖ Walk at a pace that is convenient and comfortable.
- ❖ Be very consistent with walking.
- ❖ If possible, choose a place or trail that is not noisy and where you can be exposed to nature.
- ❖ Take the opportunity to breathe deeply and walk upright.
- ❖ Use that time to pray and meditate. This is an ideal time to talk to the Creator.

Definition of the Restoration Model

- ❖ Try to appreciate nature during your walk (e.g. the stars in the sky, other celestial bodies, the vegetation, etc.).
- ❖ Drink plenty of water after each walk.
- ❖ Apart from your daily walk, consider taking the stairs instead of the elevator. Do not get upset if you can not park very close to the grocery store. Walking a little distance can only help. Use every opportunity to remain active.

S – SELF-CONTROL

'Do you not know that your body is a temple of the Holy Spirit, who is in you, whom you have received from God? You are not your own; you were bought at a price. Therefore honor God with your body." I Co 6: 19, 20

Self-control, or temperance, is necessary for everyone. Self-control applies to many areas of your life including appetite, time, ingestion of toxic substances (e.g. tobacco, recreational alcohol), speech (inability to hold ones tongue) and many other areas. To demonstrate how pivotal self-control is, consider someone who lacks self-control with regard to appetite. That individual may overeat, usually the wrong kinds of foods. The immune system is weakened. The individual becomes sickly. Sleep becomes a problem owing to heartburn. The individual becomes chronically tired. Grouchiness becomes evident. The individual becomes depressed and wants to eat even more. Self-esteem and self-image start to suffer. Everything spirals downward. This is a common scenario.

Self-control can also pertain to our speech. Some individuals that do not have a problem with appetite may instead have "*glossal dyscontrol*", i.e. they cannot control their tongue. They say things that they regret but cannot take back. This can lead to a cycle of problems affecting other individuals. Some people lack self-control with respect to anger. Their anger is unchecked. Lack of self-control with anger can be dangerous. In general, if you lack self-control (and many people do lack self-control in some form), do the following:

- ❖ Recognize that your body is not your own but God's. Realize that God's spirit is trying desperately to live in your heart, but unable to do so because of an intoxicating, unholy or unclean mental or physical environment in your body. Recognize that when God's spirit fully dwells in the temple (which is your body, your mind, and your brain) it is very difficult to remain sick, to have stress or to have spiritual dysfunctions. In other words, full restoration can be expected.

- ❖ Be aware that if *self* is not in control, something else automatically is. Always try to identify what that something is that is controlling you.
- ❖ As always if someone lacks self-control in any form, that person should ask God for help directly.
- ❖ Eat nutritiously. By following all of God's health laws, the brain and mind are able to function well. In many cases, just by following natural health laws, the problem of self-control can be taken care of without God needing to use supernatural means.
- ❖ Obtaining self-control may take time and effort. But God can certainly provide divine aid and lessen your struggle.
- ❖ Never give up!

T – TIME

"There is a time for everything and a season for every activity under heaven."
Ecclesiastes 3:1

Time is one of the greatest gifts men have. Time can be very profitable and beneficial if used wisely. When it comes to restoration, time is always an important factor. When you commit to wellness and take all of the appropriate steps toward reaching wellness, at that moment the battle is more than halfway won. Getting on the right path is just as important as reaching ones destination because given time you will get there by the grace of God.

God's timetable is different than ours. He may choose to take longer than we would prefer, or He may resolve a problem much sooner than we would ever imagine. In each case, God is the master coordinator and knows what He is doing. All we need to do is exercise patience and trust. With respect to time, we recommend the following:

Definition of the Restoration Model

- ❖ Make the right lifestyle changes now. Do not procrastinate since it will only get harder to change with the passage of time.
- ❖ Be patient, always.
- ❖ Although God's timing is different than ours, His timetable is undeniably better.
- ❖ It is more important to commit to change than to focus on the time it takes to reach ones goal.
- ❖ God does not operate in the confines of human time. Place your entire trust in Him.
- ❖ Healing takes only as long as it takes for **God's** agenda to be completed.
- ❖ God may sometimes choose to carry out His purpose during the occurrence of our affliction. This does not mean that He is the author of illness. He always has our best interests in mind though it may not always seem that way.
- ❖ Focus on the present when it comes to the necessary health changes you need to make. But focus your attention on the future to envision your eventual state of wellness.

O – OBEDIENCE

"As obedient children, do not conform to the evil desires you had when you lived in ignorance." 1Peter 1:14

Obedience is crucial when it comes to restoration. Unfortunately, disease does not discriminate between willful disobedience and one that stems from ignorance. The end result of disobedience to the natural health laws is the same. Because illness is a personal matter, it is imperative that each individual take responsibility for learning everything necessary regarding their health. Obedience may prevent illness completely.

The first place to start is with obedience to God's laws, spiritual, physical and mental. God's all inclusive laws are designed to provide optimal health in all areas. Adam and Eve were given instructions on the type of foods to eat that would allow proper function not only of their body but also of their mind. This would allow them to properly commune with their maker, the most important aspect of wellness.

Definition of the Restoration Model

When it comes to health, disobedience can have harmful consequences, sometimes severe ones. The consequences may be immediate or they may be delayed and insidious in their onset. It is however never too late to start obeying. It is also important to realize that:

- ❖ Obedience, in general, is a safeguard against self-destruction and harm.
- ❖ Health laws come in one package that must be kept entirely.
- ❖ Obedience involves trust and confidence that the health laws given are beneficial. Natural laws are restorative. However, never confuse nature with the God of nature. Only God is infallible and omnipotent.
- ❖ Obedience to proper health laws is voluntary but only temporarily so. You can choose to obey now or be forced to obey later.
- ❖ Obedience to health laws is synonymous with health promotion, health maintenance and disease prevention. None of these are passive acts. Effort is required.
- ❖ Obedience to health laws may be viewed as an investment for future wellness.

R – REST

"There remains, then, a Sabbath-rest for the people of God"
Hebrews 4:9

Rest in all forms is important. Without adequate rest, full restoration is impossible. When resting or relaxing, one can recuperate physically, mentally, and spiritually which leads to restoration. There are in fact several types of rests:

1- Sleep. Sleep is very important because it allows reparation of the wear and tear encountered throughout the day. During deep sleep important hormones are released such as growth hormones and leptins which are important in metabolism and weight management. The brain, which never shuts off, is at least able to rest during deep sleep, when blood flow to the brain and metabolism slows down considerably. With proper sleep, one is invigorated and mentally refreshed. Sleep deprivation can cause or exacerbate a variety of problems

Definition of the Restoration Model

including, seizures, migraine headaches, mood problems, memory disturbances, concentration difficulties and stress. We recommend:

    a. Get at least eight hours of sleep daily. The exact amount will vary between individuals.
    b. Go to bed a few hours before midnight. *An hour of sleep before midnight is worth several hours of sleep after midnight.*
    c. Avoid going to bed on a full stomach, in a noisy environment or after consuming caffeinated products. All of these can interfere with the quality of sleep. Invest in a comfortable mattress.
    d. It is easier to get a good night sleep after a busy and physically active day than one during which you were idle.
    e. If you have difficulties falling asleep, contact your physician. Instead of settling for a sleeping pill, try to find out the underlying cause of your sleep disturbance.

2- Relaxation. Proper relaxation can be a powerful agent to combat stress. The mind cannot stay in overdrive all of the time. Without adequate relaxation, chronic stress, mood dysfunction and anxiety symptoms may develop, not to mention cognitive difficulties. Somatic symptoms can also become evident if you consider that stress normally produces chemicals that affect several organs of the body (heart, brain, gut, lungs and muscles).

3- Sabbath rest. Just as we require daily rest, the Bible teaches the necessity of having a weekly rest called the Sabbath. This is a type of rest that provides spiritual renewal and to which a blessing is attached (see Exodus 20: 8-11).

A – ACCOUNTABILITY

"Nothing in all creation is hidden from God's sight. Everything is uncovered and laid bare before the eyes of Him to whom we must give account."
Hebrews 4: 13

When it comes to illness, you must first understand your condition. Do not hesitate to take responsibility when you know you are at fault. Poor diet, a stressful lifestyle,

Definition of the Restoration Model

lack of exercise, chronic anger and other negative emotions can all be the culprits. Acknowledging ones shortcomings is the first step in restoration. Only after a problem has been identified, can appropriate steps be taken to prevent or correct it.

You do not need to be a medical doctor to understand the fundamentals of health and illness. It is advisable to know everything that pertains to your own health and safety. It is in fact a solemn responsibility to understand the steps necessary to ensure wellness. It is the same concept with a car. You do not have to be a mechanic to know when to get your car a tune up, or to know the importance of using oil, water and the right type of fuel. Many people take much better care of their cars than their bodies. We recommend the following:

- ❖ Try to identify the cause of your illness.
- ❖ Look closely at the following factors:
    - o Your diet
    - o Stress
    - o Your relationships with other people
        - This includes family members, relatives and friends.

- Do you have a lot of enemies? Why? How are your emotions affected?
  - Spiritual life
    - Are you humble and forgiving?
    - Do you trust in God?
    - Is there is a sense of purpose in your life?
  - Self-image/self-worth/self-esteem
  - Activity level
- ❖ Decide to take action today
  - Seek appropriate help
  - Address any life-style and nutrition issues that may be present

Never procrastinate when it comes to your health.

T – TRUST IN GOD

"Trust in the Lord with all your heart and lean not on your own understanding; in all your ways acknowledge Him, and He will make your paths straight."
Proverbs 3: 5, 6

Trusting in God is the pivotal point of the RESTORATION model. There are several

Definition of the Restoration Model

reasons why, according to this model, it is important to trust in God:

- ❖ He created man; therefore, He knows and understands the source and solution to all our infirmities.
- ❖ God is omnipotent (all powerful). He can recreate, remodel, repair, and cure our illnesses.
- ❖ God has only *our* best interests in mind, all the time. He is the only one that truly understands our best interests.
- ❖ By placing our full trust in God's ability to heal us, we manifest faith, which is imperative when it comes to healing.
- ❖ You must have faith since 'without faith, it is impossible to please God" Hebrews 11:6
- ❖ The components of faith are:

    - o **F- FEAR** the Lord, shun evil and live uprightly.
    - o **A**-Do not be afraid to **ASK**. Be bold in your request.
    - o **I**- Be **INSISTENT**.
    - o **T**-Have unwavering **TRUST** in God. Respect <u>His</u> **TIMETABLE.**
    - o **H**-Only then can you expect **HEALING** and total RESTORATION

Trusting in God involves surrendering to God's will. That process is healthy and can provide peace. When healing occurs, it is important to give praise to God and to be thankful. If you really have faith, you can start the praise and thanksgiving before the healing is manifested.

I – INSIGHT

"For I know my transgressions, and my sin is always before me."
Psalm 51:3

Insight, hindsight and foresight should all go together. It is the responsibility of each individual to consider possible mistakes made in the past, assess the present, and take informed steps to ensure future wellness. Be your own medical detective.

It is a fact that the majority of patients, who seek medical help today, do so for problems that are related to lifestyle and nutrition. Many of these conditions are entirely preventable, and can be managed naturally. Understanding the source of the problem thoroughly and taking steps to correct it is

Definition of the Restoration Model

vital. It is important to *want* to get well and to be prepared to take the appropriate steps required.

Many individuals seek medical help when they are very concerned about a health problem. When you go for an office visit or to the hospital, I recommend the following:

- ❖ Ask the Lord for wisdom so that your physician(s) may be used by God.
- ❖ Prepare yourself in advance to relate any relevant information that the doctor may need. If you are prepared in advance, your visit will be more meaningful for everyone.
- ❖ Your doctor will most likely ask many questions. Unlike Christ, the healer who was interested in only one thing: "how much faith do you have?" Your doctor can only begin to decipher your problem when you answer the many questions that he/she has been trained to ask.
- ❖ Do not be afraid to ask any questions you may have. You should leave the visit having a good idea of the nature of your problem and have some understanding of what caused it. More importantly, you should be

given information regarding the steps needed to help you overcome your condition. Some potential red flags are:

- 'I think your problem is in your head'
  - There are many, many problems that are in fact caused by stress or psychological disturbances, but most of the time these problems are not 'faked'. Whether a problem is *in your head* or *in your body*, the cause must be diligently sought and addressed.
- 'There is nothing that can be done in your situation'.

In our opinion there is always something that can be done. Hope should never be taken away.

If you lack insight, you can always ask God and He will be only too happy to give it to you.

Definition of the Restoration Model

O – OPTIMISM

"So do not throw away your confidence; it will be richly rewarded."
Hebrews 10:35, 36

Optimism is always important. With optimism comes positive anticipation and hope. In the RESTORATION model, we believe that you can be optimistic because the ultimate source of healing is God. He is certainly not lacking in healing power, wisdom, mercy, or understanding. If you are not a believer, perhaps you are a skeptic, optimism can still play a role, although the context and benefits are different.

We have previously discussed the concept of placebo and placebo response. As mentioned earlier, a placebo is an inert substance that the patient thinks is a therapeutic drug (or therapy). The inert substance can, when taken, work just like a therapeutic agent. If a person has a headache, pain, depression or other problem and that the doctor prescribes what is believed to be an appropriate drug, by believing that the drug will help, many patients will get better, even if that drug is nothing other than a sugar pill. The reverse is also true. The belief that a pill is harmful may result in it causing a variety of 'side effects' even though the pill is an inert agent.

It has also been recognized that when a patient goes to see the doctor for a problem and that the doctor in all of his paraphernalia and god-like status, wheals his magical pen to write a prescription, the healing process begins then, even before the drug is taken. That entire doctor-patient encounter is vested in symbolism that musters and stimulates the internal healing processes via psychosomatic (mind-body) interactions.

Belief and anticipation are thus very important in altering symptoms. The same thing can be said about our emotions and mood; they can also alter bodily function in a beneficial or harmful way. *Psychoneuroimmunology* is a field of research that has shown how emotions, moods and mental states can influence the functioning of the nervous system and the immune system. Solomon, in the Bible, was ahead of his time when he said: "A merry heart doeth good like a medicine: but a broken spirit drieth the bones." Proverbs 17:22. As impressive as the placebo response is, it is no match for faith. By exercising

Definition of the Restoration Model

faith a person can effect healing for someone else who may not have faith or may not even know that someone else is exercising faith upon their behalf. Faith, prayer and belief in God all work together.

N –NUTRITION

"Then God said, 'I give you every seed - bearing plant on the face of the whole earth and every tree that has fruit with seed in it. They will be yours for food.'" Genesis 1:29

Eating nutritiously is perhaps the natural law that is most often broken. The difficulty is that there is a sort of *institutionalization of malnutrition*. What we mean is that many of the foods that are commonly available and sold are ones that are overly processed and sometimes devoid of all useful nutrients. The foods we eat from birth and throughout life should provide the building blocks necessary for growth, health maintenance, repair, healing and metabolism. We have a built-in pharmacy of drugs in our body that is stocked with natural chemicals to help with mood, memory, alertness, energy, weight metabolism, sleep, sugar control, and defense against pathogens, blood clotting and thinning, wound healing, and many other functions. Very simply stated, the quality of drugs that the body can make is based on the quality of foods we eat. Often, a person's nutritional intake is so poor that the natural drugs inside our bodies may not be synthesized properly or in sufficient quantity.

The wrong foods we eat can also cause sensitivity reactions and problems not so different from ones produced by harmful drugs. We consume various food additives (on average 10 lbs/person/year) that produce adverse effects. In addition, the processing of these foods eliminates vital nutrients which have resulted in malnourishment and nutritional deficiency states that are rampant today. Many children with neurobehavioral problems that we see have difficulties that, in reality, stem largely from malnutrition. Hydration is also a major problem. People would never consider taking a shower with coke, coffee or milk, yet they ingest these substances not realizing that this is what their bodies must use to cleanse their system internally. Water is vital for many functions in the body. The list is too numerous to mention. We recommend the following:

- ❖ Drink approximately 8 glasses of water per day (more specifically, the

Definition of the Restoration Model

amount of ounces equivalent to half of your body's weight in pounds).
- ❖ Eat plenty of raw fruits and vegetables daily (among other things, they contain live enzymes, fiber, antioxidants, minerals, vitamins, water and perhaps thousands of phytochemicals that are as yet unnamed).
- ❖ Avoid dairy products. Substitute with soy/rice based products.
- ❖ Avoid caffeinated beverages and foods (chocolate) and red drinks.
- ❖ Avoid certain food additives such as MSG, nitrates and Aspartame or NutraSweet.
- ❖ Consider taking nutritional supplements such as antioxidants, essential fatty acids, glyconutrients, minerals, phytochemicals, and vitamins.

If you are confused and overwhelmed about which foods are safe to eat and which ones may be contributing to your health problems, just consider the following:

- ✓ You can never go wrong with foods that are fresh, raw, and are life-producing (i.e. that contain live

enzymes and other essential nutrients such as fruits and vegetables).
- ✓ You should be cautious of foods that are *decorated and treated* with unsafe chemicals and dyes but devoid of useful nutrients.
- ✓ There is a difference between:

    o Corn on the cob versus corn chips
    o Fresh potatoes versus potato chips
    o Apples versus apple pie
    o Carrots versus carrot cake

Chapter 6- Conclusion

Total restoration of health is possible even if it takes a miracle. The following example is what complete restoration actually entails:

I was on-call at a medical center for the pediatric neurology service. I was asked to come urgently to see a 9 year old patient who had acutely become comatose. When I get a call like that, I start to generate a list of possible diagnoses in my mind so that I can act quickly. When I arrived at the PICU (pediatric intensive care unit), I found out that the patient had also been febrile. The patient had a full neurological evaluation and some tests including an MRI of the brain, an EEG and a lumbar puncture. We eventually diagnosed the patient as having a condition called ADEM (acute disseminated encephalomyelitis). In essence, this is a condition that results in inflammation of the brain and possibly other parts of the central nervous system including the spine. As in this case, patients with ADEM often have mental status change and, in severe cases, coma. We also found abnormalities on the

Total Restoration

EEG suggestive of underlying seizure activity.

The prognosis was not good, but it became worse. Overnight the patient started showing signs of increased intracranial pressure (increased pressure inside the skull). Eventually, neurosurgical placement of a device through the skull was required in order to monitor the intracranial pressure. The patient was on a respirator and various drugs to try to bring down the pressure. Unfortunately, all of our efforts were futile and the intracranial pressure continued to rise to the point where the consensus among all the doctors was that the child would not survive. The tracing on the intracranial monitor was alarming.

One morning as I walked into the patient's room in the PICU, I decided to evaluate the patient quickly and leave the room as soon as possible, hoping that I did not need to speak with the family. I simply did not have any good news for them. We all were convinced that the patient would die at any time. As I was evaluating the patient, the father approached me with tears in his eyes and asked me if there was anything I could do to save his child's life. He then added 'if there is anything you can do, even to call on

Conclusion

Jesus' name, please do so". I must admit that there was nothing further from my mind before he made that request. We had done everything medically to try to help this young child, and everything was failing.

I had not thought about divine intervention until the father mentioned it. I said to the father that I was willing to pray with him and his wife right there in the PICU, but first I asked: "do you believe that God can heal your child? Do you have faith?" Without hesitation, the father said yes. We held hands and I offered a short simple prayer. I asked God to please heal the child if it was His will. While I was praying, I heard some denigrating comments from some nurses about the fact that I was praying for a patient that was dying. Perhaps they felt that I was raising false hope. After my prayer, I said to the parents "it is now in the Lord's hands" and I left. When I went out to the nursing station, I was approached by a fellow neurologist who said that she saw me praying through the glass door. She said "you don't really expect your prayer to help?" She admitted that she did not believe in God. My reply was that God had the power to heal the child if He chose to do that. Then I left.

Total Restoration

Sometime later I was informed that the intracranial pressure was starting to come down. There was no medical explanation for this. But sure enough, when I came to check for myself, the pressure was progressively coming down. It kept going down until it became normal. The patient recovered quickly thereafter and awoke from the coma. In a few days the child was able to be transferred to a regular pediatric floor. The patient was eventually discharged from the hospital in good health.

I saw the patient for follow up in the pediatric neurology clinic after a few weeks. Although I was amazed at the child's recovery, I was expecting at least some residual neurological deficits. I was pleased when the parents, with a big smile, stated that the patient was doing very well. The patient was in fact doing much better than I could have ever expected. The child had no headaches, seizures, or memory problems. In fact, there were no complaints at all. The patient was doing very well in school without any problems with concentration. I then did a detailed neurological examination and found that indeed, neurologic function was intact. I was pleasantly amazed. Then the father said he wanted to relate a miracle that had happened besides the complete

Conclusion

recovery of his child. I must admit at this point, even though I was happy that God had performed a miracle on behalf of this child in answer to prayer, the skeptical side of me wondered if recovery was going to occur anyway. What the dad then told me was shocking. He said that when we prayed for the child in the PICU, the urge to smoke left him completely and instantly. He was a chain smoker for years. Since that prayer, he has never picked up another cigarette. What was amazing was that I did not know he was a smoker. So that was not included in my prayer. My petition was only for the child. Their marital problems were also healed. I realized that there was total restoration of this family. That is the type of restoration that is possible by the grace of God.

If you are unhealthy, and do not feel that you are enjoying optimal health, or if you are suffering from a chronic illness, there is still hope. God is the ultimate healer. He has provided simple health laws and natural tools that are innate and/or present in nature. These health *tools* are abundant, inexpensive, safe, effective and restorative. Following these health laws, which include proper nutrition, hydration, temperance, stress-free living, and spiritual renewal, will lead to total wellness.

Total Restoration

'Praise the Lord, O my soul and forget not all his benefits. Who forgives all your sins and heals all your diseases, who redeems your life from the pit and crowns you with love and compassion, who satisfies your desires with good things so that your youth is renewed like the eagles." Psalms 103: 2-5.

About the Authors

Drs. Jean-Ronel and Michelle Corbier are Christian physicians who are interested in wellness using an integrative approach. Drs. Jean-Ronel and Michelle Corbier are board-certified in their respective fields of Pediatric Neurology and Pediatrics. Although they are well-trained medical doctors and their studies have taken them to several medical institutions throughout the United States, they have felt the need to broaden their perspective on health and disease. In particular, their Christian faith and strong spiritual background have enabled them to incorporate biblical principles in their treatment of patients using a model that they call the RESTORATION model. This model is dynamic, natural, comprehensive, etiologic-based and curative. As a couple, they work closely in sharing their message of total wellness by incorporating it into their practice and sharing it with others. Their message is truly one of hope. A charitable ministry has been developed based on the RESTORATION model (www.drscorbier@neuropedsofal.com). Drs. Corbier have one son, Jean-Michel, and have a medical practice in Montgomery, Alabama.

To order additional copies of:

Total **Restoration**

Call 334-396-0761
Visit www.neuropedsofal.com

OR

Call 334-418-0088
Visit www.UfomaduConsulting.com

Notes

Notes

Notes

Notes

Notes

Notes

Notes

www.ingramcontent.com/pod-product-compliance
Lightning Source LLC
Chambersburg PA
CBHW031257290426
44109CB00012B/628